I HAVE MUSCULAR DYSTROPHY, AND IT'S OKAY!

Written by
Dr. William M. Bauer

Illustrated by
Mallory Hill

WestBow Press books may be ordered through booksellers or by contacting:

WestBow Press
A Division of Thomas Nelson & Zondervan
1663 Liberty Drive
Bloomington, IN 47403
www.westbowpress.com
844-714-3454

Because of the dynamic nature of the Internet, any web addresses or links contained in this book may have changed since publication and may no longer be valid. The views expressed in this work are solely those of the author and do not necessarily reflect the views of the publisher, and the publisher hereby disclaims any responsibility for them.

Any people depicted in stock imagery provided by Getty Images are models, and such images are being used for illustrative purposes only.
Certain stock imagery © Getty Images.

Interior Image Credit: Mallory Hill

ISBN: 978-1-6642-4438-2 (sc)
ISBN: 978-1-6642-4437-5 (e)

Library of Congress Control Number: 2021912589

Print information available on the last page.

WestBow Press rev. date: 09/13/2021

WESTBOW
PRESS®
A DIVISION OF THOMAS NELSON
& ZONDERVAN

I HAVE MUSCULAR DYSTROPHY, AND

IT'S OKAY!

About the Author:

Dr. William M. (Bill) Bauer is a licensed clinical counselor in the rural Mid-Ohio Valley area who was a former classroom teacher, principal, and college professor. He has worked with children and adults with disabilities all of his life and hopes that this book brings an understanding to children with disabilities, their teachers, and their classmates. Dr. Bauer was born with a severe hearing impairment.

THIS BOOK IS DEDICATED TO:

ALL PEOPLE WITH DISABILITIES WHOSE LIVES ARE SHARED IN THIS BOOK SERIES TO MAKE THE WORLD A BETTER PLACE. ALL WE WANT IS TO BE ACCEPTED AS WE ARE, HAVE FRIENDS, LIVE IN OUR COMMUNITIES AND TO DREAM AS OUR NON-DISABLED PEERS.

SPECIAL THANKS TO MY WIFE, MARY ELLA, DAUGHTER MADISON RYSER, HER HUSBAND ANDREW AND GRANDSON JACK.

#GRANTSPEED.
LOVE YOU, SON

To:

From:

Forewords:

I have had the pleasure of working with Dr. Bauer in the professional education and mental health fields for over two decades, and this book series is his latest outstanding work to help young people understand and accept differences. Each title focuses on a uniqueness and assures us that "it is OKAY!"

Dr. Stephanie Starcher
Public School Superintendent

Being different is OK! Every effort to erase stigma surrounding our differences is important. The earlier we start, the better chance we have at preventing stigma from even occurring. I had the honor of meeting Dr. Bill Bauer when I was in college, and it is no surprise his work as a mental health advocate would transpire into this series of books. I'm thankful for his commitment to celebrating our differences.

Nick Gehlfuss, MFA, Actor, film and television.
Currently, Dr. Halstead, Chicago Med.

This book series by Dr. William Bauer — my good friend Bill — fills a niche in children's literature that embraces diversity and self-esteem. This series is not only important, but extremely fun. As founder of Orphans International, I look forward to reading these stories to children of all faiths and abilities around the world. This book is indeed a living testament to Bill's own son. The world is a better place because of Bill Bauer! #GrantSpeed

James Jay Dudley Luce, Founder Orphans International Worldwide,
International Entrepreneur

HI!

MY NAME IS TRAVIS. I HAVE MUSCULAR DYSTROPHY, ALSO KNOWN AS M.D.

THERE ARE NINE TYPES OF MUSCULAR DYSTROPHY, ALL OF WHICH ARE VERY DIFFERENT.

I FOUND OUT I HAD MD WHEN I WAS IN ELEMENTARY SCHOOL. I STARTED WALKING JUST FINE, BUT THEN MY MUSCLES BECAME WEAKER. I HAD TO USE HELP FROM MY TEACHER, MY MOM AND MY DAD TO MOVE AROUND.

WHEN I WAS IN MIDDLE SCHOOL, MY MUSCLES BECAME WEAKER AND MADE IT HARD TO WALK.

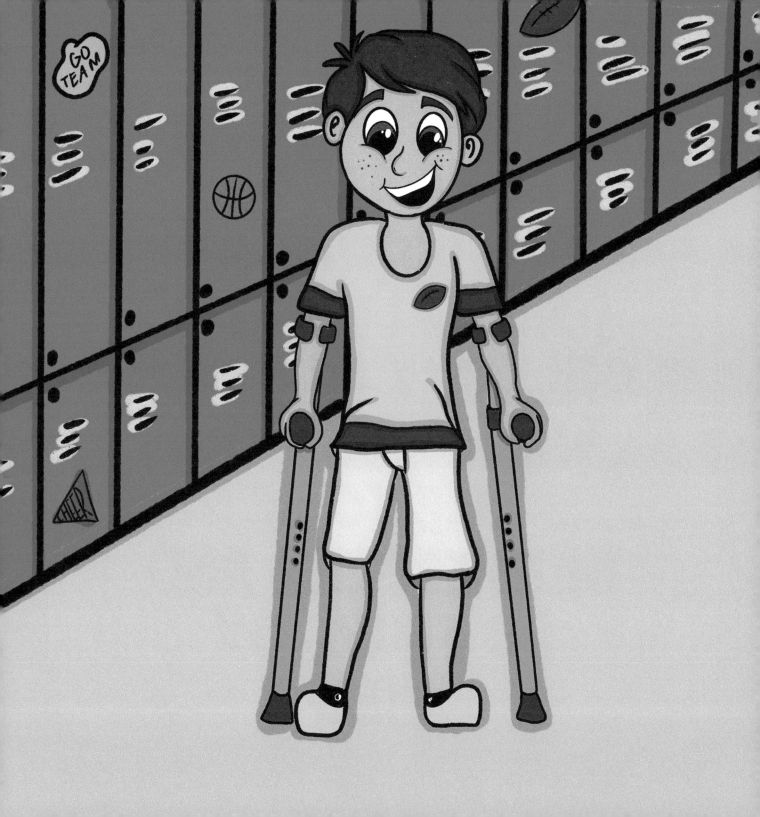

I AM IN ALL REGULAR EDUCATION CLASSROOMS AT SCHOOL. I USUALLY ONLY ASK FOR HELP WHEN I NEED IT. I LIKE TO BE INDEPENDENT AND DO THINGS BY MYSELF.

IN HIGH SCHOOL I BECAME A WHEELCHAIR USER. I AM STILL ME, I AM JUST SITTING DOWN, THAT'S ALL.

I LOVE TO PLAY VIDEO GAMES WITH MY FRIENDS, AND SOMETIMES I LIKE TO PLAY VIDEO GAMES WITH MY FRIENDS WHO ARE NOT WITH ME. THEY ARE MY "VIRTUAL" FRIENDS. I TALK TO THEM EVERYDAY. FRIENDS ARE IMPORTANT TO ME.

SOMETIMES I DROP STUFF AND RUN INTO OBJECTS. MY SCHOOL WORK IS MESSY SOMETIMES, I PREFER TO TYPE MY WORK.

SOMEDAY I HOPE TO BECOME A VIDEO GAME DESIGNER. I LOVE WORKING ON MY COMPUTER. THE COMPUTER IS SOMETHING I CAN CONTROL, WITHOUT THE WORLD CONTROLLING ME.

I HAVE NO IDEA WHAT THE FUTURE WILL BRING, BUT NOW I AM READY FOR A GOOD CHALLENGE.

MY NAME IS TRAVIS, I HAVE MUSCULAR DYSTROPHY AND IT'S OKAY!

Resources:
www.mda.org
https://www.cdc.gov/ncbddd/musculardystrophy/links.html